Jair Bol

CW00924654

From Retired Military Offi.
Brazil; his Liberal Party and WEF Controversies

By United Library

Introduction

Interested in Brazilian politics?

Jair Bolsonaro is one of the most controversial and polarizing political figures in Brazil. His biography tells the story of how he went from being a retired military officer to the 38th president of Brazil. It also covers some of the controversies he has been involved in, such as his liberal party and his appearances at the World Economic Forum.

Jair Bolsonaro was born in Brazil in 1955. He grew up in a lower-middle-class family and experienced a tough childhood. In the 1970s, he enlisted in the Brazilian Army and became a paratrooper. During his military career, he was arrested for engaging in political activity and spent two years in prison.

After his release, he founded the Liberal Party, which became one of the country's largest political organizations. However, Bolsonaro's career was marred by controversy when he was accused of participating in a financial scheme involving the sale of arms to Paraguay. In addition, his speeches often contained inflammatory language and he was accused of making racist and sexist remarks.

Despite these controversies, Bolsonaro remained popular with many Brazilians. Under his leadership, the country has experienced economic growth and rising living standards. However, Bolsonaro has been criticized for his handling of environmental issues and his close relationship with the business community.

Table of Contents

This book provides an in-depth look at one of the most fascinating and complex political figures in recent history. If you want to understand Brazilian politics, or just want to learn more about Jair Bolsonaro, this book is for you.

Jair Bolsonaro

Jair Messias Bolsonaro GOMM (Glicério, March 21, 1955) is a retired Brazilian military officer and politician, currently affiliated to the Liberal Party (PL). He is the 38th president of Brazil since January 1, 2019, having been elected by the Social Liberal Party (PSL). He was a federal deputy for Rio de Janeiro between 1991 and 2018. He was born in the municipality of Glicério, in the interior of the state of São Paulo, but lived in several other cities in São Paulo throughout his childhood. In 1966, his family settled in Eldorado, in Vale do Ribeira, where he spent his adolescence with his five brothers.

He began his military career in the Rio de Janeiro municipality of Resende, after graduating from the Agulhas Negras Military Academy in 1977. Later, he served in the Brazilian Army's field artillery and paratroop groups. He became known to the public in 1986, when he wrote an article for *Veja* magazine criticizing the military's low salaries, for which he was arrested and detained for fifteen days. A year later, the same magazine accused him of planning to plant bombs in military units, which he denied. After being convicted in the first instance, the Military Superior Court acquitted him of this accusation in 1988. He transferred to the reserve in the same year with the rank of captain and ran for the Rio de Janeiro City Council, being elected councilman as a member of the Christian Democratic Party (PDC).

In 1990, Bolsonaro was elected to the lower house of the National Congress, a position to which he was reelected six times. During his 27-year term as congressman, he became known for his social conservatism and several controversies, mainly for being a vocal opponent of LGBT rights and for statements classified as hate speech, which include the defense of torture practices and murders committed by the Brazilian military dictatorship. Regarded as a polarizing politician, his views and comments, widely described as far-right and populist, have attracted both praise and criticism in Brazil and around the world. Bolsonaro was announced as a presidential pre-candidate in March 2016 by the Christian Social Party (PSC), but his presidential campaign was launched by the PSL in August 2018, when he began presenting himself as an anti-establishment, pro-market candidate and defender of family values. After contesting the second round of the 2018 general elections with Fernando Haddad of the Workers' Party (PT), he was elected with the support of 55.1% of the valid votes.

His government has been characterized by the strong presence of ministers with a military background, international alignment with countries governed by the populist right, and anti-environmental, anti-indigenist, and pro-gun policies. Although his first year in office maintained the trajectory of slow economic growth and falling crime rates that had been recorded since the end of the Michel Temer government, his administration became embroiled in a series of controversies and several of the ministers who had originally been appointed left their posts and criticized the government. Subsequently, Bolsonaro's response to the COVID-19 pandemic in Brazil was also frowned upon across the political spectrum and singled out as a denialist, after he downplayed the effects of the disease, advocated treatments with no proven effectiveness, discouraged the use of protective masks and delayed the purchase of vaccines, In addition, he clashed with governors and fired two health ministers because he disagreed with their social distancing measures, positions that contributed to an increase of up to 400,000 preventable deaths in the total of more than 600,000 deaths recorded in the country during the pandemic. In the 2022 elections, he was defeated in the second round by Luiz Inácio Lula da Silva (PT), becoming the first president of Brazil to fail to be reelected since the institution of reelection in 1997.

Childhood

According to family accounts, Jair Bolsonaro was born in Glicério, a small town in the northwest of São Paulo state, and was registered ten months later, on February 1, 1956, in the city of Campinas, where most of his Italian and German immigrant family lived. In his birth register, however, his birthplace is recorded as being Campinas.

The name Jair was chosen after a neighbor's suggestion, in honor of Jair Rosa Pinto, left midfielder of the Brazilian National Soccer Team who had a birthday that day and played for Palmeiras, team Percy Geraldo Bolsonaro, his father, supported. Initially, he would only be called Messias Bolsonaro because his mother, Olinda Bonturi, after a complicated pregnancy, attributed the miracle of her son's birth to God.

During his childhood, he lived in several cities in the state of São Paulo. In the first years of his life, his family moved to Ribeira. After a few years, in 1964, the family moved to Jundiaí in the neighborhoods of Vianelo and Vila Progresso. In 1965, they moved to Sete Barras. Finally, in 1966, they moved to Eldorado, in Vale do Ribeira, where Jair grew up together with his five brothers. He completed high school at the Eldorado Paulista State School.

He is the third among the siblings - three boys and three girls. He hunted birds with a shotgun and earned money by fishing and harvesting palm hearts. Bolsonaro's friends nicknamed him "Palmito," but over time he became just "Mito. His nickname has nothing to do with heroic deeds of the past.

Military career

Bolsonaro says he became interested in the Army at the age of fifteen, when he and friends allegedly provided tips to the military on possible hiding places for Carlos Lamarca, who had set up a camp in Vale do Ribeira to train guerrillas against the military dictatorship.

At seventeen, Bolsonaro entered the Army Cadets Preparatory School (EsPCEx). However, after reflecting, he came to the conclusion that he should have taken the competition for the Military Academy of Black Needles (AMAN). Then, at the end of 1973, after some months at EsPCEx, he took the exam and was approved. He graduated in 1977.

At the end of his last year of academy, he joined the Parachute Infantry Brigade, where he specialized in parachuting. After completing the course, he went to serve as an Officer Aspirant in the 21st Campaign Artillery Group (GAC) in São Cristóvão, a district of Rio de Janeiro. Then, he served in the 9th GAC in Nioaque, Mato Grosso do Sul, from 1979 to 1981. In this last year, his first son, Flavio, was born. The following year, 1982, he attended the Army Physical Education School (EsEFEx) and his second son, Carlos, was born.

After graduating from school, he went to serve in the 8th Parachute Campaign Artillery Group in Deodoro, a neighborhood of Rio de Janeiro. He was one of the lieutenants responsible for the physical evaluation of the soldiers who applied for the parachuting course. In 1987, he attended the Officers Improvement School (EsAO).

Documents produced by the Brazilian Army in the 1980s show that Bolsonaro's superiors evaluated him as having an "excessive ambition to achieve financial and economic fulfillment". According to Bolsonaro's superior at the time, Colonel Carlos Alfredo Pellegrino, Bolsonaro "had the permanent intention of leading the subordinate officers, in which he was always repelled, both because of the aggressive treatment dispensed to his comrades, and the lack of logic, rationality and balance in the presentation of his arguments".

Prison

In 1986, when he was already serving as a captain in the 8th Parachute Campaign Artillery Group, Bolsonaro was arrested for fifteen days after writing, in the "Ponto de Vista" section of *Veja* magazine of September 3, 1986, an article entitled "The salary is low". For Bolsonaro, the dismissal of dozens of AMAN cadets was due to the low salaries paid to the category in general, and not to deviations of conduct, as the Army leadership wanted to make clear. The attitude of his superiors led to a reaction from active and reserve officers, including General Newton Cruz, former head of the central agency of the National Intelligence Service (SNI) in the João Figueiredo government. Bolsonaro received about 150 solidarity telegrams from various regions of the country, in addition to support from officers of the Military Institute of Engineering (IME) and wives of officers, who held a demonstration in front of the military complex at Praia Vermelha, in Rio de Janeiro. He was acquitted by the Military Superior Court (STM) two years later.

Operation Dead End

On October 27, 1987, Jair Bolsonaro informed *Veja* magazine reporter Cássia Maria about the "Beco Sem Saída" operation. At the time, Bolsonaro supported the improvement of pay and was against the arrest of Captain Saldon Pereira Filho. The operation would have aimed to explode low-power bombs in bathrooms of the Vila Militar, the Academia Militar das Agulhas Negras, in Resende, and in some other military barracks in order to protest against the low pay that the military received at the time.

Bolsonaro allegedly drew the sketch of where the pump would be placed in the Guandu Pipeline, which supplies water to the municipality of Rio de Janeiro. The magazine delivered the material to the then Minister of the Army, who, after four months of investigation, concluded that the report was correct and that the captains had lied. The Military Justification Council (CJM) unanimously considered, on April 19, 1988, that Bolsonaro was guilty and that he should be "declared incompatible for the oficialacy and consequent loss of rank and patent, in the terms of article 16, clause I of law no. 5.836/72". In his defense, Bolsonaro claimed at the time that *Veja* magazine had published fraudulent accusations to sell more with sensationalist articles.

The case was handed over to the Military Superior Court (STM). The trial was held in June 1988 and the court accepted the defense's thesis that the documentary evidence - whose expert report was made by the Army Police - was insufficient because it did not allow handwriting comparisons, since handwriting in block letters was used. The STM absolved the two officers, who were thus maintained in the Army's ranks. Still in 1988, Bolsonaro went to the reserve, with the rank of captain, and in the same year, he began his political career, running for councilman in Rio de Janeiro. The Army Police report, however, would later be corroborated by the Federal Police, which confirmed Bolsonaro's handwriting.

Alderman of Rio de Janeiro

In 1988, he entered public life by being elected a councilman in the city of Rio de Janeiro for the Christian Democratic Party. According to his son Flávio's biography, Bolsonaro "was a candidate for city council because it happened to be the only option he had at the time to avoid being a victim of persecution by some superiors. His entry into politics happened by chance, because he wanted to continue his military career. He assumed his mandate in 1989, staying only two years in the Municipal Chamber of Rio de Janeiro. During his mandate, he presented seven bills, one of which authorized free transportation for military personnel on urban buses. His mandate as councilman was mainly used to give visibility to military causes.

Bolsonaro proved to be a conservative councilman, discreet and with little participation. In one of the few speeches he made in plenary, he complained about a note published by the newspaper *O Dia,* which accused him of recording the speech of fellow councilors with attacks on the Armed Forces to send to the military. On other occasions, Bolsonaro defended birth control: "there is no point in coming with palliatives, showing leaflets to the poor population that is illiterate," he said. He also considered ineffective the distribution of condoms to slum dwellers, because "the kids will play with bladder", and said that the containment of population explosion should occur "over the humble class". The councilman's words were transcribed in the City Council Journal, because at the time the House did not have a television channel.

Federal Deputy

In the 1990 elections, he was elected federal deputy, also for the PDC. This was to be followed by another six successive terms. In addition to the PDC, he was affiliated to eight other parties throughout his political career: PPR (1993-95), PPB (1995-2003), PTB (2003-2005), PFL (2005), PP (2005-2016), PSC (2016-2017), and the PSL (2018-2019), In 2017, he stated that he had already thought about joining Prona, also coming to talk about his affiliation to PEN, now Patriot, but nothing materialized.

While deputy, Bolsonaro also ran for the presidency of the House of Representatives. In February 2017, Bolsonaro ran for the third time for the position of president of the House of Representatives, obtaining only four votes. He had previously run for the same position in 2005 and 2011, and was defeated in all those attempts.

In the House of Representatives, Bolsonaro was a member of the Foreign Relations and National Defense Committee and the Public Security and Combating Organized Crime Committee, and alternate member of the Human Rights and Minorities Committee. In March 2005, Bolsonaro was decorated by President Luiz Inácio Lula da Silva with admission to the Order of Military Merit in the rank of Special Grand Officer. Bolsonaro gave up his bid for an eighth re-election as a congressman in order to run for the presidency of the Republic in 2018.

Projects

According to a survey of the newspaper *O Estado de S. Paulo*, in 26 years of activities in Congress, Bolsonaro presented 171 bills, complementary law, legislative decree and proposed amendments to the Constitution (PECs), being rapporteur for 73 of them. According to Lupa Agency

- which gives the total number of projects as 172 - 162 of these were bills (PL), one was draft supplementary law (PLC) and five were proposals to amend the Constitution (PEC); there are 470 other proposals submitted by the deputy, but these are not bills: they are amendments to proceedings in committees, indications of authorities to provide information in cases considered by the House, and messages and manifestations in plenary.

Bolsonaro managed to approve two bills and one amendment: a PEC that provides for the issuance of receipts along with the vote in electronic ballot boxes; a proposal that extends the benefit of exemption from the Tax on Industrialized Products (IPI) for computer goods and another that authorizes the use of phosphoethanolamine, a substance that became known in Brazil as the "cancer pill" and that tests have shown to have no effect against the disease. Bolsonaro justified the approval of a single amendment claiming that he does not receive enough support from other members of Congress because he suffers "discrimination" for having right-wing ideals.

In the case of ballot boxes, the amendment proposes printing a voucher, which is verified by the voter at the printer and then deposited, by the machine itself, in a sealed ballot box. He defends this system to prevent fraud in vote counting and because there is "no country in the world" that uses Brazilian technology, insinuating that the electronic ballot boxes are vulnerable. Although the system is tested periodically and has never been corrupted, some experts question its defenselessness. According to the Superior Electoral Court (TSE), the proposal would generate additional costs of about 1.8 billion reais to public coffers. In June 2018, the Supreme Court (STF) decided to overturn the printed ballot in the 2018 elections because it considered that this could generate a risk of breach of secrecy and freedom of choice, by the possibility of clerks needing to intervene in case of failure of printing.

Bolsonaro was the author of a Proposal of Amendment to the Constitution (PEC) that provides that the Unified Health System (SUS) performs sterilization and vasectomy surgeries on people over 21 years who wish to undergo the procedure. He argued that many poor families do not have money to make surgeries like these and would have difficulties in performing their family planning for this reason. This agenda, however, was already defended by him since the early 90s, when he was a councilman.

Bolsonaro also presented PL 1 411/2011, which decharacterizes as a crime the refusal, in religious temples, to accept or perform ceremonies or people in disagreement with their beliefs and liturgies.

Candidacy for the Presidency of the Republic

Jair Bolsonaro ran for the presidency of the Federative Republic of Brazil for the Social Liberal Party in the 2018 presidential elections with General Mourão (from PRTB) as vice-president, in the "Brazil above all, God above all" coalition. His candidacy, which had two challenges, was unanimously granted by the Superior Electoral Court (TSE).

Jair Bolsonaro was the first presidential candidate to reach the amount of one million reais in campaign donations through crowdfunding. The amount was reached after 59 days from the beginning of the campaign, on July 5, raising an average of seventeen thousand reais per day. On August 23, he began his campaign, enjoying strong police protection and wearing a bulletproof vest. The then president of the PSL, Gustavo Bebianno declared that Bolsonaro was at maximum risk level.

Attack

On September 6, 2018, Bolsonaro was the victim of a knife attack during a campaign in Juiz de Fora, Minas Gerais. He was hit in the abdomen and had to undergo an exploratory laparotomy procedure at the Santa Casa de Misericórdia de Juiz de Fora. Adélio Bispo de Oliveira, identified as the author of the crime and later arrested, declared, in the police report, that he did it "on behalf of God". Adélio was affiliated to PSOL between 2007 and 2014; the party issued a statement classifying the attack as "a serious attack on democratic normality and the electoral process". After the attack, he had two surgeries and was discharged in late September. Bolsonaro's stabber was arrested, tried and acquitted. Bolsonaro said he would appeal the decision, however the sentence has become res judicata.

On the day of the attack the other presidential candidates Álvaro Dias, Ciro Gomes, Geraldo Alckmin, Guilherme Boulos, Henrique Meirelles, João Amoêdo, Marina Silva, Cabo Daciolo, João Goulart Filho and Vera Lucia repudiated the attack through social networks. The president of the Republic, Michel Temer, classified it as "intolerable". Former President Dilma Rousseff referred to the attack as regrettable and linked the motivation of the crime with opinions held by the candidate.

Manifestations

On September 29, 2018, using the *hashtag* #EleNão, a movement started on social networks by women opposed to the candidate's proposals gathered expressive street demonstrations during the 2018 presidential campaign. The demonstrations were attended by about five hundred thousand people, according to the organizers of the event, and took place in more than 160 cities in all states of the country and also in cities such as New York, Barcelona, Berlin, Lisbon and Paris.

On September 30, acts of support for the candidate were organized. In Brasilia, the campaign organized a motorcade with 25,000 cars, according to the Military Police. In São Paulo, a rally took over four blocks of Paulista Avenue, but no official figures were released. According to the event's organizers, the number reached 1.8 million, an unrealistic estimate, since in a previous demonstration for the *impeachment of* Dilma Rousseff, which occupied the entire avenue, Datafolha estimated an agglomeration of five hundred thousand people. On October 21, the Brasil Livre and Vem Pra Rua movements also organized acts against the Workers' Party (PT) throughout Brazil.

Electoral performance

He obtained 49 276 990 votes in the first round of the election, which took place on 7 October, corresponding to 46.03% of the valid votes, being the most voted of the round. As no candidate reached 50% of the valid votes, the Superior Electoral Court called for a second round of voting between Jair Bolsonaro and Fernando Haddad of the Workers' Party (PT). Jair Bolsonaro won in sixteen states and the Federal District, exceeding 50% of the vote in thirteen states.

On 28 October the second round of the election took place, and Jair Bolsonaro confirmed the result of the first round, obtaining 57,797,847 votes (55.13% of the valid votes), thus successfully electing himself the 38th president of the Republic in Brazil. Bolsonaro repeated his victory in fifteen states where he had won in the first round and also in the Federal District, but was unable to maintain his victory in Tocantins.

Bolsonaro interrupted the cycle of four consecutive victories by the Workers' Party, which had been repeated since 2002, when Luiz Inácio Lula da Silva won the presidential election that year. Bolsonaro is the tenth military man to become president of the Republic, the first since the beginning of the New Republic. He is also the first Italian-Brazilian directly elected to the presidency of the Republic. Other Italian-Brazilians who have held the office of president were Ranieri Mazzilli and Itamar Franco, who were interim presidents; and Emilio Garrastazu Medici, indirectly elected president during the military dictatorship.

Republic Presidency

On October 11, days before his victory at the polls, Bolsonaro announced Congressman Onyx Lorenzoni (DEM) as the future head of the Civil House in his office.

On October 31, already as president-elect, Bolsonaro announced astronaut Marcos Pontes as the future Minister of Science and Technology. In addition to Pontes, Bolsonaro had already made two other ministerial appointments: Paulo Guedes as Minister of Economy and Augusto Heleno, a reserve general, as Minister of Defense. The latter, however, was later appointed to the Institutional Security Cabinet of the Presidency on November 7.

On the first day of November, Bolsonaro confirmed that Judge Sergio Moro had accepted his invitation to serve as Minister of Justice and Public Security. The decision generated backlash from the international press because Moro had convicted Luiz Inácio Lula da Silva, Bolsonaro's main opponent in the election, of money laundering and corruption.

On January 1, 2019, Jair Bolsonaro and Hamilton Mourão were sworn in as president and vice president of the Republic in a ceremony at the National Congress. After the event, Bolsonaro received the presidential sash from the hands of former President Michel Temer and made a speech in the parlatory of the Planalto Palace. Bolsonaro's inauguration had the largest security reinforcement in the history of inaugurations, with about six thousand agents and 2,600 military police.

Economy

Bolsonaro has defended developmentalist economic positions, voting with the Workers' Party on several economic issues. In 2000, for example, when explaining to host Jô Soares why he advocated the "firing squad" of then-president Fernando Henrique Cardoso, he said that "barbarity is privatizing Vale and telecommunications, handing over our oil reserves to foreign capital". Since presenting himself as a presidential candidate, however, he has supported liberal economic measures. However, he voted in favor of opening pre-salt exploration, stated that the "free-market is the mother of freedom", that "as much as possible should be privatized" and only opposed the way in which Vale was privatized.

In May 2018, he defended the flexibilization of labor rights and stated "that less rights and employment is better than all rights and unemployment. In an interview in August 2018, however, he said he "would not like" to privatize Petrobras, but would do so if "no other solution can be found". After assuming the presidency, Bolsonaro appointed Paulo Guedes to head the Ministry of Economy, created by merging the ministries of Finance, Planning, Development and Management, Industry, Foreign Trade and Services and part of the Ministry of Labor.

In 2019, the first year of the Bolsonaro government's mandate, Brazil's GDP grew 1.2%, followed by a 3.9% drop in 2020, mainly due to the impacts of the COVID-19 pandemic in Brazil, when the country dropped out of the list of the ten largest world economies for the first time since 2007. In 2021, the economy resumed growth with a 4.6% increase in GDP, but IMF expectations for 2022 are for slow growth of 0.8%. In the period between 2019 and 2021, the unemployment rate went from 11.9% to 14.4%, double the world average (ILO data), while the inflation rate went from 4.31% to 10.06%, the highest in six years.

International relations

During the 2018 presidential campaign, Bolsonaro said he would make considerable changes to Brazil's international relations, saying the country should stop "praising dictators" and "attacking democracies." Bolsonaro made his first international trip as president to Israel, while stating that the state of Palestine "is not a country, so there should be no [Brazilian] embassy" and that it "does not negotiate with terrorists."

Bolsonaro is a big supporter of former US President Donald Trump. and is considered the most pro-American candidate in Brazil since the 1980s. During an October 2017 campaign rally in Miami, Florida, he saluted the United States flag while shouting "USA! USA!" to a large crowd.

At the regional level, he praised former Argentine President Mauricio Macri for ending the twelve-year regime of Néstor and Cristina Fernández de Kirchner, which he considered similar to Lula and Rousseff. Although he has no plans to leave Mercosur, he criticized the bloc for considering that it prioritized ideological issues over economic ones. A staunch anti-Communist, Bolsonaro also condemned the current regime governing Cuba.

Despite having shown distrust of China throughout the presidential campaign, claiming that the Asian country "[wants to] buy Brazil." he stated that he wished to continue doing business with the Chinese.

Environment

The president even considered the possibility of extinguishing the Ministry of Environment, an idea that gained momentum in November during the transition government, but backed off the decision. However, the Environmental Education department of the Ministry of

Environment was incorporated by the Secretariat of Ecotourism, while the Brazilian Forest Service was transferred from the Ministry of Environment to Agriculture.

During the month of August 2019, fires in the Amazon became the focus of intense criticism of Bolsonaro's policies for the rainforest area. Brazil recorded more than 72 000 fires in 2019, an increase of 84% over the same period in 2018. In five days in August, there were 7,746 fires. The concern prompted Angela Merkel to back Emmanuel Macron's request to put the fires in the Amazon on the agenda of the G7 summit, after the French president said the situation represented an international crisis. In response, President Jair Bolsonaro - who has ironically called himself "Captain Chainsaw" - accused Macron of having a "colonialist mentality" and told him to stay out of Brazilian business.

After that, the Bolsonaro government launched a global public relations campaign to try to convince the world that everything is under control. Bolsonaro said that "in my understanding it may have been potentiated by NGOs, because they lost money, what is the intention? Bring problems to Brazil" pointing out that Leonardo DiCaprio "gave the money" to burn the Amazon. In 2021, the president came out in defense of Minister Ricardo Salles, who was under suspicion of committing crimes of corruption, administrative advocacy, prevarication and facilitation of smuggling.

The Bolsonaro government's environmental policy has been intensely criticized by scientists and experts in the field, describing it as extremely damaging to the environment, but it is supported by several agribusiness and mining sectors. Environmental legislation has been widely eroded; regulatory and oversight structures including the Ministry of Environment, Funai and Ibama have lost powers and have been scrapped; funding for the sector has been reduced; he dissolved the Climate Change Secretariat; he stopped applying most of the resources available in environmental funds, cut 93% of the budget for research on climate change; he promised in his campaign to end an alleged "environmental fine industry", and in his government the application of fines has been almost completely paralyzed. The president has attacked indigenous peoples, environmental institutions and NGOs, and has disseminated much false or distorted information to justify his policies.

Under his government deforestation in the Amazon grew by 56.6%, levels in 2021 were the highest since 2006, and between 2019 and 2021 the country lost 42,517 km^2 of forests, triggering negative impacts on the environment, biodiversity, climate, population, agriculture, the economy and Brazil's image abroad. Most of the deforestation occurred to enable the expansion of agriculture and cattle ranching. Land grabbing, logging, mining, mining and invasions of indigenous lands were also important causes. A large part of deforestation is done by burning. The president accused indigenous and traditional peoples of promoting the burnings, and claimed that they can also be the result of spontaneous fire, disagreeing with scientific studies. Bolsonaro has also disseminated distrust of satellite data on deforestation collected by the National Institute for Space Research, and promoted denialism about the problem of global warming. His policies threaten the fulfillment of Brazil's international commitments to reduce greenhouse gas emissions. The international repercussion of his actions on the environmental and climate issue has been largely negative.

Education

The Bolsonaro government has prepared a bill to regulate homeschooling in Brazil, with minimum requirements that parents or legal guardians must meet, such as registration on a platform to be developed by the Ministry of Education and the possibility of evaluation. In 2018, however, the Federal Supreme Court (STF) decided not to recognize homeschooling because there is no constitutional provision on the subject in the country. During the discussion in the STF, the Office of the Attorney General of the Union (AGU) and the Office of the Attorney General of the Republic were against *homeschooling*.

On April 3, 2019, the then Minister of Education, the Colombian Ricardo Vélez, said that history textbooks would undergo a revision so that children "can have the truthful, real idea of what their history was" and cited as examples the coup of 1964, which he classified as 'constitutional', and the military dictatorship, which he said was 'a democratic regime of force'. The minister's speech angered the military dome for creating 'unnecessary wear and tear'. On April 8, 2019, Vélez was dismissed from the MEC.

At the end of April, the new management of the Ministry of Education, under Abraham Weintraub, announced a 30% block in the budget of federal educational institutions, among the sixty universities and almost forty institutes throughout the country. Initially, the minister had announced the cut of funds of UFF, UFBA, and UnB, which, according to him, "are making a mess". Subsequently, the cut was extended to all federal universities. According to the National Association of Directors of Federal Institutions of Higher Education (Andifes), the contingency reached 20% of the budget for costing (ie, maintenance services, cleaning, security, among others), and 90% of the investment budget. In May, the MEC announced that it was also studying to "decentralize" investments in philosophy and sociology courses, which mobilized a manifesto against the proposal signed by representatives of prestigious universities worldwide, such as Harvard, Yale, MIT, Oxford, Cambridge, Sorbonne, Columbia and Berkeley.

Minister Milton Ribeiro, the fourth to hold the portfolio, served from July 16, 2020 until March 28, 2022. Shortly after his departure from the Ministry, in June 2022, Ribeiro was arrested and accused of passive corruption, prevarication, administrative advocacy and influence peddling, allegedly organizing a "parallel cabinet" composed of evangelical pastors who had a say in the distribution of federal education funds and mediated meetings with officials. The scandal became known as the "Bolsolão of the MEC. After the case was publicized, ten mayors denounced pastors' schemes in the MEC.

Since 2019 universities have lost 25% of their budget. The government cut almost R$ 5 billion from the Ministry's 2021 budget, and in 2022 it cut 2.4 billion. In 2021 the budget allocated 220 million for early childhood education, in 2022 the allocation fell to 100 million, and for 2023 2.5 million were provided. In addition, in 2019 the MEC failed to apply almost 7.9 billion of the authorized value for basic education, and in 2021 did not execute 6 billion. The government's actions in the field of education have received much criticism, being accused also of not seeking dialogue with students, civil society and local governments; of attacking and persecuting teachers and researchers; of promoting the defamation of educational institutions; and of interfering in university autonomy.

According to researchers Ximenes & Lindquist, "the low education budget, cuts and precarious execution were a hallmark of the Bolsonaro administration in the Ministry of Education. From Abraham Weintraub justifying that there was no cut, but 'contingency', to Milton Ribeiro claiming that the improvement in Brazilian education 'is not a matter of money', the budget discredit permeated the various changes in the command of the MEC. This scenario of neglect of the education budget is consistent with the fragility of educational policies and the evidence of corruption that put the MEC in the headlines. For the Association of University Professors of Bahia, "the poor performance of the Bolsonaro government in education is proven by the numbers, with his government showing worsening in virtually all indices. [While in the most developed countries teachers of all levels are valued by society, in Brazil there has been a reversal in recent years. The networks of hate, stimulated by programs such as Escola Sem Partido, by digital militias such as MBL and by politicians like Jair Bolsonaro have led part of society to systematically attack education professionals".

Culture

The Bolsonaro government extinguished the Ministry of Culture along with the Ministries of Sports and Social Development, being the three merged into the structure of the Ministry of Citizenship. After the announcement, Culture secretaries from eighteen states launched a manifesto calling for the maintenance of the body. On January 1, 2019, from the administrative reform of the newly sworn-in government, the MinC was officially extinguished by Provisional Measure No. 870, published in a special edition of the Official Gazette of the Union. Within the Ministry of Citizenship, the Secretariat of Culture was created, which was later transferred to the Ministry of Tourism.

On July 19, 2019, Bolsonaro stated that if the government cannot impose some "filter" on Brazilian audiovisual productions through the National Cinema Agency (Ancine), he would "extinguish" the agency, which can only happen with the approval of Congress. Bolsonaro also said he intended to transfer the agency's headquarters from Rio de Janeiro to Brasilia and criticized the use of public money to make "pornographic films", such as "*Bruna Surfistinha*'s", in addition to having defended that national cinema should now talk about "Brazilian heroes". Bolsonaro's statements about Ancine caused negative repercussions in the sector. Two of the biggest film and entertainment magazines in the United States, *The Hollywood Reporter* and *Variety,* dedicated articles to Bolsonaro's threat to extinguish the agency and his comment about the need to create "filters" in the selection of films that the agency supports. On August 2, however, Bolsonaro declared he might back down from his decision to extinguish Ancine because the "audiovisual sector employs a lot of people".

In August, after Ancine's then-director and president, Christian de Castro, was removed from office by judicial decision, Bolsonaro said he wanted a "terribly evangelical" name to replace him. On January 16, 2020, Roberto Alvim, the then special secretary of Culture, posted a video on social media in which he paraphrased excerpts from a speech made to theater directors in 1933 by Joseph Goebbels, minister of Propaganda of Nazi Germany. Moreover, during the video in question, the background music was the opera *Lohengrin*, by composer Richard Wagner, also associated with Nazism.

COVID-19

Since the beginning of the COVID-19 pandemic in Brazil, Bolsonaro has issued several controversial statements ranging from denialism and omission of the number of deaths claiming they are not in the proportions scientifically recognized by the World Health Organization, to even claims considered pseudoscientific about protective measures, such as the use of protective mask, social distancing and bioimmunization with the use of vaccines, questioning their effectiveness and Chinese origin. Bolsonaro also fired two health ministers in less than a year for disagreeing with social distancing measures and because they did not defend treatments without proven effectiveness.

After participating in demonstrations in favor of himself that occurred on March 15, 2020, Bolsonaro said that, although worrying, there is an "oversizing" and "hysteria" regarding the coronavirus situation. He was criticized by several authorities for the attitude of breaking isolation and going to the streets, which was called "attack on public health" by Rodrigo Maia, president of the House of Representatives, and "inconsequential" behavior by Davi Alcolumbre, president of the Senate.

On March 18, Bolsonaro responded to the criticism by saying: "I as head of the Executive, the Brazilian nation's greatest leader, have to be at the front, next to my people. Do not be surprised if you see me, in the coming days, entering the crowded subway in São Paulo (SP), entering a barge on the Rio-Niterói crossing at rush hour; or on a bus in Belo Horizonte (MG)...". This stance proved contrary to the recommendations of the Health Minister, Luiz Henrique Mandetta, who always advocated social isolation to prevent the rapid growth of cases of infection by the virus and who was fired by Bolsonaro because of it.

On March 17 and 18, there were demonstrations against Bolsonaro in several Brazilian capitals due to the government's stance on the pandemic. There were also, in much smaller numbers, demonstrations in favor of Bolsonaro. The act was repeated between March 19 and 21. In a statement on March 19, he said that the acts are part of "democracy" and that it will not be a "little flu" that will bring him down. On two occasions, Bolsonaro also imitated people with shortness of breath to refer to patients with COVID-19.

In April, Nelson Teich was appointed as the new Minister of Health. In May, however, Teich resigned from the Ministry of Health after being contradicted by Bolsonaro about the use of chloroquine and social distancing measures.

In June, Bolsonaro again downplayed the severity of the pandemic and threatened to leave the World Health Organization (WHO). In July, after fever, muscle pain and malaise, Bolsonaro tested positive for coronavirus. However, he reported that his fever had decreased, attributing the improvement to hydroxychloroquine. In the same month, he showed a box of chloroquine to emus living in Alvorada Palace, as well as riding a motorcycle without wearing a mask, talking to garbage men while he was contaminated. For his posture in facing the disease, he received, along with eight other presidents, the 2020 IgNobel Award for Medicine Teaching, a satirical and humorous award granted to unusual discoveries.

In December, Bolsonaro, criticizing the contract for the purchase of the vaccine from Pfizer, said that if the vaccine turned people into "crocodiles" or "bearded women", the company would have no responsibility. The president's speech gained international repercussion and became the butt of jokes.

In October 2020, after Governor João Doria announced a partnership between Instituto Butantã and Chinese company Sinovac for the production of Coronavac, a vaccine against COVID-19, Bolsonaro forced Eduardo Pazuello, the third person appointed to the position of Health Minister in less than a year, to cancel the purchase of the vaccine within the federal government. Bolsonaro has criticized Coronavac repeatedly, questioning its effectiveness and Chinese origin, as well as celebrating when the trials were briefly suspended due to the suicide of one of the participants. In November 2020, when the country surpassed 160,000 deaths, Bolsonaro again made controversial statements, claiming that Brazil "has to stop being a country of faggots."

In January 2021, Bolsonaro announced that his government would purchase doses of Coronavac, despite his intense campaign against the immunization. The National Health Surveillance Agency approved AZD1222 and Coronavac on January 17, the same day vaccination began in Brazil, in a ceremony held by the government of São Paulo. The arrival of the Oxford/AstraZeneca vaccine was delayed, and on January 18, Bolsonaro called Coronavac "the vaccine of Brazil," reversing its previous label that it was "João Doria's Chinese vaccine." In this context, the start of vaccination in São Paulo was significant political failure for Bolsonaro.

After the collapse of Manaus hospitals in January 2021, Bolsonaro became the target of protests of the population. Also intensified, in the demonstrations, the calls for *impeachment,* both the population, as politicians of the right and left. Due to the crisis in Manaus, 119 deputies (Network, PSB, PT, PCdoB and PDT) filed a request for *impeachment* against the president.

In late February 2021, Brazil reached the mark of 250,000 deaths by COVID-19. A few days later, with the pandemic registering a rapid increase in deaths and the health system of several states in collapse, Bolsonaro declared: "Enough of this freshness, of mimimi. How long are you going to keep crying?"

In early May, the president reported that "the military knows that [the coronavirus] is chemical, bacteriological and radiological warfare" On May 21, Bolsonaro was fined by the Maranhão state government for not wearing masks and causing crowding. Two days later, he participated in a parade with motorcyclists through several neighborhoods of Rio de Janeiro. The president, who in the previous days claimed to have again felt symptoms of COVID-19 and to have taken chloroquine to "prevent the disease," did not wear a mask, as did most of the event's participants. That same week, Bolsonaro stated that the health minister would draft an opinion to dispense with the mask requirement, but then stated that the decision would be up to local authorities and the minister himself. On June 17, the president argued that contracting the virus was more effective than the vaccine itself.

Because of Bolsonaro's stance on the pandemic, the CPI of COVID-19, a parliamentary commission of inquiry investigating alleged omissions and irregularities in the Bolsonaro government's spending during the COVID-19 pandemic in Brazil, was created on April 13, 2021 and officially installed in the Federal Senate on April 27, 2021. On July 2, 2021, the Attorney General's Office asked the Supreme Court to open an inquiry to investigate Bolsonaro for the possible crime of prevarication in the case of overbilling of the Covaxin vaccine, in a spin-off of the investigations conducted by the COVID-19 CPI.

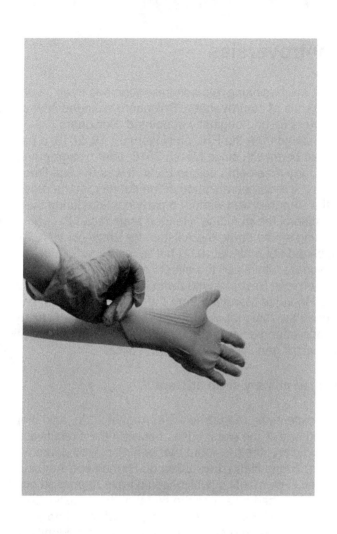

Controversies

Since the beginning, his administration has been involved in a series of controversies. Bolsonaro changed nine of the ministers he had originally appointed. Bolsonaro disaffiliated from the PSL on November 19, 2019, a party he had been with since March 2018, after disagreements with party president Luciano Bivar. It was the first time since the redemocratization of the country, that a president of the Republic was without a party caption during the exercise of the mandate. He then announced the project of creating a new party, the Alliance for Brazil (ALIANÇA), which did not materialize. In his second year in office, Bolsonaro minimized the effects of the COVID-19 pandemic in Brazil, clashed with governors, fired physician Luiz Henrique Mandetta from the Ministry of Health and caused the resignation of Sergio Moro from the Ministry of Justice after dismissing Maurício Valeixo from the position of director general of the Federal Police.

Alleged military coup attempt

An article in the magazine *Piauí* August 2020, said that during one of the worst crises between the executive and the judiciary, the president met behind closed doors with Walter Braga Netto, Luiz Eduardo Ramos and Augusto Heleno. The meeting, which would have happened on 22 May 2020, had as a fuse the fact that the minister Celso de Mello consult the Attorney General's Office to know whether or not to order the seizure of the president's cell phone and his son, the then councilman Carlos Bolsonaro.

Bolsonaro wanted to send army troops to the Supreme Court because the justices, in his opinion, were overstepping their bounds in their decisions and diminishing their authority. Upon reaching the Supreme Court, the idea was that the military would dismiss the current eleven justices and the replacements, military or civilian, would then be appointed by Bolsonaro, staying in office "until that is in order," in the president's words.

In an attempt to calm the spirits of the president, the chief minister of the Cabinet of Institutional Security Augusto Heleno, who is also a reserve general in the Brazilian Army, wrote a note on his *Twitter* account on the same day in which he cited the events and made veiled threats to the Supreme Court. The note generated great repercussion and several criticisms both from civil society and from entities and congressmen.

Candidacy for the Presidency of the Republic 2022

Jair Bolsonaro's 2022 presidential campaign was made official on July 24, 2022 in Rio de Janeiro. The vice on the slate was Walter Braga Netto as the federation candidate. In the Oct. 2 first-round vote, his opponent Lula was the front-runner with 48.43 percent of the electorate. Bolsonaro qualified for the second round receiving 43.20% of the vote. On October 30, the second round of voting, Bolsonaro was defeated by Lula.

Personal life

Jair Bolsonaro was married three times. His first wife was Rogéria Nantes Nunes Braga, whom he helped to elect as a city councilor in 1992 and 1996, and with whom he had three children: Flávio (senator from Rio de Janeiro), Carlos (like his father and mother, city councilor of Rio de Janeiro, the youngest in the country) and Eduardo. He divorced and, from his second marriage, with Ana Cristina Valle, he had Renan.

In 2007, he met his current wife, Michelle de Paula Firmo Reinaldo, when she was a parliamentary secretary in the Chamber of Deputies. Nine days after being hired, the two signed a prenuptial agreement and, two months later, they were married on paper. In 2013, the couple had a religious ceremony performed by Pastor Silas Malafaia. With Michelle, the deputy had his first daughter, Laura. The family lives in Alvorada Palace.

Bolsonaro claims to be Catholic, but claims to have attended the Baptist Church for ten years. In 2016, he was baptized in the Jordan River by an evangelical pastor from the Assembly of God. His current wife, Michelle, and their children are evangelicals.

Genealogy

Bolsonaro is a descendant of Italian and German immigrants, with probably a more remote Portuguese origin as well. On his mother's side, Bolsonaro is of Italian descent, and his grandparents were both born in the city of Luca, in Tuscany. On the paternal side, he is great-grandson of Italians from Veneto and Calabria, and also has a great-grandfather from Hamburg, Germany. The original spelling of the surname was Bolzonaro. According to Jair Bolsonaro's own statement, his great-grandfather was German and was a soldier in Adolf Hitler's Wehrmacht during World War II: "He had no choice: either he was a soldier or he was a wall", he declared. However, according to the genealogy presented, Carl "Carlos" Hintze, Bolsonaro's great-grandfather, was born in Germany around 1876 and arrived in Brazil as a child in 1883, five decades before the start of the Second World War in Europe, so he was 54 when Hitler came to power and 69 at the end of the Second World War, without there being any evidence that he left Brazil during this period. His German great-grandfather died in Campinas on 16 March 1969.

Health

In July 2020, Bolsonaro contracted COVID-19 - he was then involved in a series of controversies surrounding the disease, such as saying it was "a little flu", that because of "his history as a [army] athlete" he would not get seriously ill and for appearing in public without a mask. Three weeks after the first examination, the tests continued to come back "positive", and by the end of the month, the illness had developed into pneumonia, which he publicly called "mold on the lung".

In early September 2020, media reported that he would undergo a procedure to remove kidney stones.

On July 14, 2021, Bolsonaro was admitted with intestinal obstruction at the Hospital das Forças Armadas (HFA), in Brasilia, and was transferred on the same day to São Paulo, where he was treated at the Vila Nova Star hospital. He was discharged on July 18, 2021, having the press reported that surgery was ruled out due to the evolution of the condition.

On January 3, 2022, he felt strong abdominal pains while he was resting on the coast of Santa Catarina during the year-end recess, in the midst of the crisis caused by the floods in southern Bahia in 2021. Subsequently, he was flown by helicopter to the city of São Paulo, where medical exams indicated the occurrence of a new episode of intestinal obstruction, requiring hospitalization so that the appropriate treatment could be administered.

Accusations of corruption

In a 1999 interview on a Bandeirantes network program, the deputy said: "My advice and I do it: I evade everything possible. The name of the then deputy is registered on the so-called Furnas list, a corruption scheme that used cash money to fuel 156 political campaigns in 2000. Although the congressman claims that the list is false, its authenticity was proven by a Federal Police report.

A report on the website *Vice* brought the issue to light in March 2017 due to the repercussions of Operation Weak Meat. The politician posted a video on his YouTube channel, where he explains that the two hundred thousand reais, half the amount spent on his campaign, were returned as "donation to the party". However, in the TSE spreadsheet, the same value (two hundred thousand reais) back to Bolsonaro account, but this time in a donation made by the party fund.

On April 7, 2020, the *Sportlight Agency* revealed invoices showing that Bolsonaro, when a congressman, overbilled reimbursement of public funds for fuel. At the end of the month, Minister Luiz Fux, of the STF, referred a criminal notice to the Attorney General's Office against Bolsonaro.

In December 2017, the newspaper *O Globo* reported that the deputy and his sons employed a former parliamentary wife and two of her relatives in public positions in their offices. According to the newspaper, these people occupied the vacancies from 1998. However, as the hirings occurred before 2008, when the STF normatized the rules against nepotism, they cannot be legally classified as such. A *Folha de S.Paulo* report, made in January 2018, denounced that the deputy hired a ghost servant in Brasilia. According to the article, between January and June, Walderice Santos Conceição received more than seventeen thousand reais as an employee of the parliamentary office in the House of Representatives, but worked as an acai seller in the municipality of Angra dos Reis, in Rio de Janeiro.

In September 2018, *Veja* magazine published an article with details of a lawsuit with more than five hundred pages filed by ex-wife Ana Cristina Siqueira Valle against Bolsonaro. In the lawsuit, filed in April 2008 in the 1st Family Court of Rio de Janeiro, amid a contentious separation, Ana Cristina made several accusations against Bolsonaro, including: concealment of assets before the Electoral Justice in the 2006 election, incompatibility of income with his monthly earnings and theft of cash and jewelry from a safe in a branch of the Bank of Brazil. After the allegations, the IRS opened an investigation in 2008, but found no irregularities. After the disclosure of the report, Bolsonaro sent a request to the Public Ministry of Rio de Janeiro, requesting the withdrawal of circulation of issue 2602 of *Veja* magazine. He also asked, in the request, the investigation of how the report had access to a process that was filed and processed in secret from Justice. Later, Ana Cristina claimed to have lied to the Justice in her statement.

In 2019, Public Prosecutor's Office of the State of Rio de Janeiro opened investigation proceedings of possible money laundering and concealment of assets of the former parliamentary aide Fabrício Queiroz and Senator Flávio Bolsonaro on account of financial transactions in which eight employees of Flávio's office made deposits totaling 150 thousand reais in Queiroz's account, always on dates after the payment of salaries, which raised suspicions that the parliamentarian misappropriated part of the servers' salaries, illegal practice known as "rachadinha". One of Queiroz movements mentioned by the report is a check 24 thousand reais issued in favor of first lady Michelle Bolsonaro, justified by Jair Bolsonaro as "payment of a loan of forty thousand reais". On August 23, 2020, when questioned by a reporter from Grupo Globo about the deposits made by Fabrício Queiroz in the first lady's account, Jair Bolsonaro threatened the reporter by responding, "My will is to fill your mouth in the beating." The episode had wide negative repercussions, including internationally.

In December 2020, President Jair Bolsonaro was named "Corrupt Person of the Year" by the Organized Crime and Corruption Reporting Project (OCCRP), an international consortium of investigative journalists. The award "recognizes the individual or institution that has done the most to promote organized criminal activity and corruption in the world. According to the organization, Bolsonaro won for "surrounding himself with corrupt figures, using propaganda to promote his populist agenda, undermining the justice system, and waging a destructive war against the Amazon region that has enriched some of the country's worst landowners.

Decorations and awards

In April 2019, Bolsonaro was selected by *Time* magazine as one of the 100 most influential people in the world that year and described him as a complex character. On the one hand he would represent a break in a decade-long string of corruption and the "best chance in a generation" to pass economic reforms that can tame the growing debt. On the other hand, the magazine highlighted Bolsonaro's controversial character, describing him as a symbol of "toxic masculinity" and "homophobic ultraconservatism" that could even reverse Brazil's progress on climate change.

Awards

- 2019 Person of the Year" by the Brazilian-American Chamber of Commerce.
- One of *Time* magazine's 100 most influential people in 2019 and 2020.
- 2019 Brazilian-American Chamber of Commerce Person of the Year.
- 2020 OCCRP Person of the Year "for his role in promoting organized crime and corruption."
- On October 25, 2021, Bolsonaro was recognized as an honorary citizen by the City Council of Anguillara Veneta, Italy, the hometown of his paternal grandfather. This sparked reactions in Italy.

Liberal Party

Partido Liberal (**PL**), formerly known as **Partido da República** (**PR**), is a right-wing Brazilian political party founded and officially registered in 2006. It currently holds the largest seat in the chamber of deputies. As a member of the so-called "Centrão", the party is a support base of President Jair Bolsonaro's government, as it was of former presidents Lula, Dilma Rousseff and Michel Temer. In February 2022, the party had 761,415 members, making it the eighth largest party in the country. Its president is Valdemar Costa Neto.

History

The Party of the Republic united the Liberal Party (PL) and the Party for the Reedification of National Order (PRONA), which merged in 2006 in order to surpass the 5% threshold for votes required at the time, a challenge made difficult by the party's involvement in the Mensalão scandal, which had become public the previous year. Also in this context, the PL lost the vice-presidency of the Republic with the disaffiliation of José de Alencar, who had been elected in 2003 on Luiz Inácio Lula da Silva's ticket. Despite this, the party remained in the government's base.

In the 2012 elections, it elected 3110 councilors nationwide, and in 2014, it elected 40 federal deputies.

Sergio Victor Tamer, founder of PR, was president of the party from 2006 to 2014. Alfredo Nascimento succeeded Tamer as president of the PR until April 2016, when he resigned due to the party leadership did not support the impeachment of Dilma Rousseff. However, 26 deputies PR voted for her impeachment.

Following this move by its deputies, the party quickly left its bipartisan past and supported Geraldo Alckmin's failed campaign in the 2018 Brazilian presidential election.

On May 7, 2019, the Superior Electoral Court (TSE) authorized the Republic Party (PR) to change its name back to the Liberal Party (PL).

In the 2020 elections, the party won 345 mayorships and elected 3467 councilors, without electing any mayors in the capital cities.

In 2021, the party received the membership of President Jair Bolsonaro and several of his supporters.

In the 2022 general election, the party formed a presidential slate and many slates for governors with a right-wing coalition with the Republicans and Progressives.

Controversies

The Superior Electoral Court (TSE) released a dossier on October 4, 2007, with the parties with the most parliamentarians removed for corruption since 2000. The PL occupies seventh position in the *ranking*, with seventeen cassations, behind the DEM, PMDB and PSDB, PP, PTB and PDT. The party also received campaign donations from contractors privileged by its administration in the Transport Ministry portfolio.

It was seen as controversial that Jair Bolsonaro joined, in 2021, the party of Valdemar Costa Neto, arrested in the Mensalão scandal (criminal action 470), along with deputy Bispo Rodrigues and a former treasurer of the PL (Jacinto Lamas).

*

See all our published books here:
https://campsite.bio/unitedlibrary

CPSIA information can be obtained
at www.ICGtesting.com
Printed in the USA
BVHW031559091222
653840BV00011B/1530

9 789493 311558